WHISPERS, DREAMS, MEMORIES

JOHN THOMAS SERPA

Copyright © 2016, 2020, 2024 by John Thomas Serpa

All rights reserved.

No portion of this book may be reproduced in any form without written permission from the publisher or author, except as permitted by U.S. copyright law.

Cover & Interior Design by Jourdan Dunn

Dedicated to my son

MATT

WHISPERS, DREAMS, MEMORIES

INTRODUCTION

This book grew form life experiences while living in Tracy—a small farming and "blue collar" town in Northern California. It reflects the interactions to the ever-changing realities of life while living in small town America. These poems display many different styles of poetry but the concentration is not based on style or complexity, but rather on the emotion each poem brings.

ACKNOWLEDGMENTS

I would like to thank Mr. Danny Dunne (San Joaquin Delta College English teacher) for his encouragement and support. Thanks also to my Aunt Josephine, who taught perseverance, humility, and love.

In Dreams	1	Green And Gold	55
The Magical Journey	3	Like A Knife	57
Butterfly	5	On My Shoulder	59
The Hour Glass	7	Bakersfield Blues	61
In the Wind	9	Knowing Love	63
Wrapped Up In Time	11	To The Sea	65
From Father To Son	13	The Savage Beast	67
Just A Free Soul	15	Here By Me	69
New Lovers Dance	17	Murder One	71
Wild And Free	19	The Unknown Hero	73
A Soldier's Son	21	Forever	75
Shooting Star	23	Don't Follow Me	77
Summers Turn To Fall	25	This Kind Of Love	79
Vengeance	27	Blue Collar Man	81
Hand Of God	29	Bad Love	83
Inside Of Me	31	The Spider's Web	85
For Us All	33	Hold Me	87
Another Chance at Love	35	Did You Ever Wonder	89
Seashells In The Sand	37	A Dying Breed	91
Yesterday Once More	39	Tough Girl	93
Street Fighter	41	Small Town Circles	95
To Be Loved	43	Sometimes	97
Higher Ground	45	Old Love	99
Rainbows	47	Ready to Die	101
True Love	49	Quotes	103
It's Tuesday	51	My Little Hometown	105
That Very Moment	53		

In Dreams

The beauty of her face
Comes to me in dreams

Skin of golden brown honey
Eyes, dark and commanding
Hair flowing in springtime wind
And scent of garden flowers
Imagination takes me like a thief
As we lay down side by side

The beauty of her face
Comes to me in dreams

Falling, falling into her arms
And mostly out of my mind
Her warm heart covers me
Like a blanket during winter
We laugh and dance into forever
As suddenly we're frozen in time

The beauty of her face
Comes to me in dreams...

The Magical Journey

This life's magical journey
Of worry and strife
To trust in the future
And find purpose and fight

This life's magical journey
Of dark clouds and pain
To seek out the sunlight
And learn to laugh in the rain

This life's magical journey
Of hatred and sin
To find only the truth
And know love will always win

This life's magical journey
Of memories and dreams
To live every day grateful
And hope heaven is all it seems

Butterfly

To chase the fleeting butterfly
Knowing it will always get away

To find the oceans' biggest wave
Knowing it will soon disappear

To write love letters in the sand
Knowing they will be washed away

To search for that one shooting star
Knowing it will fade into the darkness

To wish the day would last forever
Knowing we will never be here again

To teach me these lessons in life
Knowing heaven was taking you away

The Hour Glass

The hour glass is dripping fast, but you are
grieving about the past. White grains of
sand roll down your face. Time to
get back in the race. Life isn't
always what it should be.
Now go and find your
destiny. Lost love
has put you
in a rage,
and now
here comes
middle age. Your
winter is not here.
Don't be a prisoner to your
fears. Hurry now to your goals.
Your life's calling will be told. Find
what you need to do. A new beginning
waits for you. The hour glass is dripping fast.

In The Wind

Strong gusts blow
From far away
The lonely pain
of yesterday

The message clear
Within the wind
Looking back
Is but a sin

Feel it now
The gentle breeze
Lifting courage
From its knees

And if you listen
It brings by
A new life
For you to try

For there is love
In the wind
Always waiting
To come again

Wrapped Up In Time

As you look up beyond the sky
It's only natural to wonder why

And when you question the unknown
Just you remember you won't be alone

The pain that you now feel
Is only the journey to help heal

And friends are standing near
If only to lend an ear

The comfort will come with the breeze
And look like fond memories

And the tears of grief will bare fruit
That grow into honor and tribute

So weep and pray or shout out loud
The sun is there behind the clouds

And if questions weigh heavy on the mind
The answers are just wrapped up in time

From Father to Son

My son, you don't understand
What happens between a woman and a man

Daddy left and you don't know why
I know you know I'm not a bad guy

It's something we had to do
Sorry we put this burden on you

When you ask me to stay the night
Saying no, hurts me deep inside

The loss of time with a son
Is too much for any father

But I'll keep trying
And see you when I can

Someday you will see
You're everything in the world to me

They can take our time
But they can't break our spirit

I will have a happy life
With you the biggest part of it

I will be father, brother, and friend
And our happiness will have no end

And when it's all said and done
You will feel this special Love

From Father to Son

Just a Free Soul

Just a free soul
Strolling through God's land
Loving us along the way

Such a soft touch
Caressing us with
So much tenderness

Just a happy face
Smiling all the time
Brightening up our day

Such a yearning mind
Trying to please everyone
Although taking from no one

So now time goes on
Your fiver of love
Will never run dry

All we have is so many memories
Of happiness with you
Always to be with us

So it is said that all things must pass
Yet in the hearts of your family and friends
Your unique quality of love will be eternal

New Lovers Dance

New lovers dance
A brutal game of chance
Get golden rings
Buy expensive things
Future looks bright
Baby sleeps at night

Changes without warning
Layoffs by morning
Stress and bills
Little white pills
Blame goes around
Picket fence comes down

Lies and schemes
Big lawyer machine
Money's all gone
Life moves on
Pain deep within
Promise of never again

Strangers at the bar
Flirting by the car
Didn't learn a thing
Now looking for rings
New lovers dance
A brutal game of chance

Wild and Free

A long time ago it was me and you
And all the crazy things we would do

Those days we can't get back
In Corvettes and Cadillacs

We really thought we had it all
Concerts, girls, and ballroom brawls

Cruising for late night fun
The cops had us on the run

Parents were giving us the big frown
Hoping someday we'd settle down

Living our lives without a care
Broken promises and love affairs

Never thinking about giving in
We were brothers thick and thin

Midnight Harley Davidson rides
For each other we would die

We were the best of friends
Thinking those days would never end

A Soldier's Son

Raised by a war hero
A long time ago
Put behind a machine gun
At just twelve years old

No time to question
Or understand
The disciplined ways
Of a military man

Always taught to
Stand my ground
For that is where
Courage is found

I studied Joe Fazier
And the great Bruce Lee
The fear of death
Was never meant for me

In a ballroom brawl
Late one night
Five men attacking
Still needed a knife

The lonely road
I chose to take
Ended somewhere
Between pride and hate

Even now as time
Eats up the days
It's still difficult
To change my ways

And with only God
On which to lean
I will not bow
To any earthly king

So when it's all
Said and done
I remain grateful
A soldier's son

Shooting Star

Strength and looks and long flowing hair
Approaching life without a care

Never worry, living fast
Couldn't wait to have a blast

Seeing what others couldn't see
With only the goal of being free

No one to stop you it would seem
In this, your American Dream

Your restless spirit needed to soar
They couldn't hold you anymore

Always dancing across the moon
The future gone way too soon

Now they only love you from afar
This shiny fleeting shooting star

Vengeance

A broken heart
Lovers well know
Awakens the monster
Inside the soul

A tortured man
With no one to blame
Yet this demon lives
Within the veins

From this world
There is no shame
Where only fools
Call your name

Just a ghost
I can't shake free
Bringing a life
Of misery

Oh sweet vengeance
The drug that I crave
You come so quickly
To dance on my grave

Summers Turn To Fall

Songs on the radio
Memories unfold
A summers love
The gift from above

Picnics at the park
Whispers in the dark
One quick glance
Back seat romance

She loves so easily
More than a fantasy
This little heart of gold
Won't let me go

Changes come too soon
A dark hospital room
Life not what it seems
Left now only to dream

The best of times
Float across the mind
But you can't relive it all
Because summers turn to fall

The Hand of God

The reflection now is real
With no time left to heal

Beautiful memories won't last
Once destiny has been cast

The victories are no more
Now facing death's door

But acceptance you don't choose
Even with nothing left to lose

So fight on now if you must
Till the bones turn to dust

The pride is too blind to see
The light of tranquility

And the courage is just a fraud
When running from the hand of God

Inside of Me

For every tick of the clock
And your beauty that never stops

For every hour of the day
Wondering if you would stay

For all we used to do
Isn't enough to hold you

For all the mistakes made
And the reasons you went away

For if only I knew
This empty life without you

For if only you could see
The pain left inside of me

For Us All

Dead leaves blowing
Off the trees
True love fading
To the past
Blood keeps dripping
From the guns
Strong ones taking
From the weak
Poor souls starving
In the streets
Black greed flowing
From the sea
Good hearts praying
In the night
Future crumbling
For us all

Another Chance at Love

Just a simple picture sent my way
As curiosity gets me through the day

Maybe an invitation or playful tease
Still it took me to my knees

Hopeful thoughts of what could be
As daydreams bring new life to me

It's only a crush from a forgotten past
But still the heart beats fast

Maybe a misunderstanding at its best
Yet my imagination will not rest

I try to calm the storm inside me
But she pulls me in so easily

One thought of her and no one else exists
Didn't know I was ready to take the risk

Is this just a silly fantasy?
Or is there another chance at love for me

Seashells in the Sand

Walking hand in hand
Looking for seashells in the sand

Rocks, crabs, and sand dollars
Was that a seal or an otter

Teasing the waves that come to greet
Hoping the cold water doesn't catch our feet

Laughing and holding on tight
The waves pull the sand with such might

Relaxing and having a picnic
As we watch surfers do their tricks

Gazing at the horizon
As we are hypnotized by the ocean

Nighttime on the beach
And the rest of the world is out of reach

Snuggled up to the warm fire
Sharing our dreams and desires

Then we pack and sneak away
Memories of a lifetime in one short day

A happier time I don't remember when
I love being with you and looking for

Seashells in the sand

Yesterday Once More

Through the looking glass of time
We take this journey in our minds

Many years and broken dreams later
Reuniting and eager to remember

Speaking fondly of school days gone by
When our young spirits soared so high

We embrace the joy and not the sorrow
As yesterday replaces tomorrow

The bonds that were made long ago
Bring nourishment to the soul

We thank those that helped us
Pay tribute to those gone before us

And if for just a handshake or a smile
It is worth it all the while

So let's laugh and dance, and remember
Those good ol' days forever

And once again let our spirits soar
As we pretend it's yesterday once more

Street Fighter

I walked into a bar at 21 years old
When a man said I looked too bold
Before I could walk away
There was a beer bottle coming my way

From then I knew how it would be
You got to fight to be who they want you to be
As I got tougher I realized
You can fight without knowing why

I can't remember which fights I've won
But now they've got knives and guns
Before I could turn around one night
They took my friend's dear life

You can win and yes, you can lose
Now it's a different road I must choose
The fights will go on and on
Another name for the guy that won

Now that I'm a little older
People say I'm a little colder
But society has molded meanness in me
Because I remember how it used to be

To Be Loved

To walk with you in the countryside
And feel this is where I belong

To roll together in the tall green grass
As if today is all that matters

To run down a mountainside
Being free, yet wanted

To watch a running stream
As our hopes flowing in our minds

To lie underneath the afternoon sun
And feel the warmth in your heart

To be in your arms as the sun sets
While the wind rushes through your hair

To hope the day would never end
Knowing tomorrow you'll still be here

To be loved, it's happening to me
And I hope you feel it too

Higher Ground

Should have known better this time around
Red flags were laying on the ground

Angry past lovers, someone should pay
Here was my chance to walk away

Saying I better get myself in line
Other lovers are waiting this time

One more verbal jab to the chin
Never to pass this way again

Bitterness looks so small in the rear view mirror
Hope answers are found to the fears

Through the pain, peace is found
Time to forgive and move to higher ground

Rainbows

I like the colors of rainbows
And gazing at the stars
On a clear summer night

I like running on the beach
And falling asleep in the sand

I like smelling wild flowers
And raindrops running down my face

I like candlelight dinners
And listening to jazz music

I like romantic nights
And laying by the fire

But most of all
I like being with you

True Love

My true love went by so fast
You moved away from your past

Lost contact with all your friends
Thought I would see you again

Time will not quiet today
The memories of yesterday

Wanting now as I reach the end
To see that pretty face again

Ready to take the final ride
Hoping you will be on the other side

Where did you go? No one would say
As I take my last breath today

It's Tuesday

On Wednesday I went to your game,
You weren't there when I called your name.

On Thursday I got the runaround,
And you were nowhere to be found.

Friday you went to get something to eat,
Saturday they tell me you're asleep.

Sunday I get the bad news,
Even though it's my day to see you.

Monday I can't wait to see,
What excuse is waiting for me.

It's Tuesday and I miss my son.
The games after divorce have begun.

That Very Moment

Pretty as the break of day
As suddenly she came my way
But untold pain of long ago
Left a bitter taste in her soul
In desperation she played the field
Yet her heart would not yield
Men were faceless in this game
Never again to cause her pain

I listen and try to understand
And show her I'm a different man
And first she runs and hides
As excuses take up her time
But I just wait and see
If she has any love left for me
We kiss and she goes off into a stare
Thinking maybe he really does care

Once when I was holding her one night
She said I love you without a fight
As she lays with tears in her eyes
She's ready to give love another try
I now know love is not win our lose
But a feeling we do not choose
And if I could stop time this I would do
That very moment she said I love you

Green and Gold

The slow drifting of the mind
To a friendly place in time

On the football field we stood
Where only the toughest could

The captain, it was made clear
Would take us through the fear

In bloody battles we hoped to see
The Bulldogs tasting victory

The glory would come in swirls
From the prettiest of the girls

And everyone would know
The one they called the hero

Now the future long ago cast
This yearning of the past

For it is here I choose to stay
Forever frozen in yesterday

Being young and strong and bold
And wearing colors of green and gold

Like A Knife

The tongue like a knife
Bored little housewife

To your face a disguise
Cuts you down with lies

Stone fly from a glass house
At night quiet as a mouse

Spreading pain onto others
From someone else's covers

If the husband only knew
Secrets aren't meant for two

Don't care who's brought down
Karma is waiting to be found

Trapped in an evil little life
Beware the tongue like a knife

On My Shoulder

Out from the shadows with a friend
Love not always until the end

Betrayal has taken a bite from me
Hatred like blood is all I see

Seeking guidance from up above
Never knew the dark side of love

Revenge boils out from the veins
No time left for guilt or shame

Temptation drags me through the sand
Prison walls are waiting for a broken man

Can't have regrets when I'm older
But the devil dances on my shoulder

Bakersfield Blues

Springtime love affair
Magic everywhere
The future is ours
Hearts in the stars
Life's a dream
My beauty queen

Foolish mistakes
Rumble like earthquakes
The devil dances
At second chances
Run away or stay
Oh yesterday

A moment in time
The years not mine
Loneliness flies
In the midnight skies
Never made it through
The Bakersfield blues

Knowing Love

The belt snaps hard
The skin breaks easily
The little boy cries

The pain comes again
The family looks away
The secret is now safe

The wounds take time to heal
The scars will last forever
The boy grows up knowing hatred

The boy becomes the father
The precious gift is his
The lessons of life unfold

The belt stays in the drawer
The father hugs his child
The little boy smiles

The cycle has been broken
The wounded heart mends
The boy grows up knowing love

To The Sea

The beauty of the northwest coast
Spirit changing for most
And from the sunny beach
A new romance is within reach
Just a glimpse and it seems
Enough to make a dream

Even the dolphins look to see
This goddess in front of me
The sharks swarm to no avail
Of the sea this holy grail
And in this moment of time
They would know she is mine

Disappearing now from above
Unable to return to love
Deep from the water within
The heart sill to mend
The mind plays tricks on me
For mermaids belong to the sea

The Savage Beast

This time taken by surprise
I guess no reason to ask why

So much done and much to do
Never thought it would be this soon

Working many hours day and night
Carried your burdens with such might

A man of great discipline and love
I shake my fist at Heaven above

Nothing to you was ever hard
Even the changing of the guard

Wondering now what to do
All those that depended on you

Knowing your spirit is never gone
Your quiet voice says carry on

Big brother you will never know
The image you left in my soul

Oh Death, the Savage Beast

Here By Me

She came into my home,
Looking for a man to call her own.
She came into my heart,
Knowing it was torn apart.

She came with arms open wide,
Filling me with joy and pride.
She came for love and happiness,
And brought grace and tenderness.

She came in the nick of time,
To give me peace of mind.
She came for a place to feel free,
And that place is here by me.

Murder One

It happened one night at a local bar
When one man went way too far

I should have known when he turned his back
That he was planning a sneak attack

One quick knife to my friend's chest
And he would take his last breath

Next I would see my with own two eyes
A Father's rage and a Mother's cries

There's nothing that can bring back a son
So what good has a plea bargaining ever done

A broken family with endless tears
All this coward got was a couple years

Can't believe the injustice that was done
A cold-blooded killer got away with murder one

The Unknown Hero

Late at night, hoping for the best
A life is being put to the test

On the outside everything looks fine
As negative thoughts control the mind

The war on depression has begun
But many battles have already been won

Not wanting to cause any shame
Trying so hard to mask the pain

It's nothing serious, they say
But the suffering doesn't go away

Never willing to make a fuss
Much stronger than the rest of us

This champion that no one sees
Fights to conquer negativity

Yes, heroes come and heroes go
But this one, most don't even know

Forever

My worries vanished
My pain lifted
My prayers answered

My purpose clear
My spirit proud
My future bright

My eyes gleaming
My heart opened
My blood yours

My love unending
My life meaning
My son forever

Don't Follow Me

You fill my body with pain
As illness comes my way

You slow my metabolism
And steal my discipline

You take my dear mother
And without warning, my brother

You eliminate my employment
And toy with my finances

You cloud my mind with stress
As I become one of the homeless

You are a predator standing still
Wanting to go in for the kill

Yet I know somehow I will get away
Death, don't follow me today

This Kind of Love

It's time to make everything just right
As I reach to turn out the light

Clothes and fears are pushed aside
As our fantasies go for a ride

No time left to feel any shame
As we light our romantic flame

I awaken your senses within
As you helplessly give in

Desires out of control and ready to burst
As we quench our undying thirst

Love and lust all wrapped in one
Complete satisfaction when it's done

In the morning we yearn once again
Hoping this kind of love never ends

Blue Collar Man

What he goes through to make ends meet
Endless hours working on his feet

You can't tell by the look in his eyes
The pain is covered with too much pride

Another layoff and it's time to go
There's not much left to show

Very little retirement or pension plan
But he won't ask for a helping hand

Day after day he gives his best
and only in his grave will he rest

His hands are cracked, his back is aching
But his soul is not for the taking

He will die with a shovel in his hand
It is the life of the blue collar man

Bad Love

Love me
Not true
Bad love
I'm through

Want sex
Pass time
Real love
Not mine

Don't care
Hate men
That knife
Goes in

Selfish love
Want it all
Crazy fool
Take the fall

Miss me now
Too late
Lost soul
It's your fate

Love me
Not true
Bad love
I'm through

The Spider's Web

Just past the midnight hour
She shows her greatest power

Sneaking up on her victim at will
Slowly going in for the kill

Planning ahead for what's about to be
Crawling in the bed so easily

In the darkness she goes to work
Lust is the poison you just took

Spinning the head around just for fun
As lies roll off her tongue

You're playing asleep with a quiet yawn
Ready to escape at the break of dawn

Yes you can heal the wound
But you will never be immune

So heed the call when it is said
And don't go near the spider's web

Hold Me

Smiling
Touching
Kissing

Sensation
Anticipation
Expectation

Whispers
Dreams
Memories

Now and then
Tight and close
Soft and real

Moments of pleasure
Feelings of joy
Peace of mind

Did You Ever Wonder

What makes a rainbow
The mountains so high
The beauty in the clouds
What's beyond the sky

What makes a friend turn
A lover leave, a mother cry
Why is true love so rare
Does anyone really care

What does the future hold
Is greed the only way
And war the answer
Will we all be destroyed

What makes a rainbow
The mountains so high
The beauty in the clouds
What's beyond the sky

A Dying Breed

On the shores of a Hawaiian paradise
Kamikaze pilots came raining down
The call of war rang out
To a small California town

Leaving the family farm behind
The first one to go
Ready to give up his life
With freedom the only goal

The Marine Corps became like his father
The American flag, his mother
And the M1 rifle, a trusted friend
Like no other

On the sands of Okinawa
In a far away land
They took a Portuguese farm boy
And made him a killing man

In a time when the word hero
Was left only for a chosen few
And uncommon valor was expected conduct
Of the Red, White, and Blue

His heroes never were presidents or kings
Yet his fellow soldiers that drank from his canteen
Months in a rat hole full of mud
Victory was spelled with the spit of his blood

He returned a hardened man of grit and steel
Never to complain, never to yield
A survivor of war, master at blocking out pain
As time goes by he would do it all again

And in the waning years, no real surprise
Refusing to take the ambulance rides
A simple salute is all he would need
As we say goodbye to the last of a dying breed

Tough Girl

She says she's been hurt before
And not going to take it anymore
She doesn't need a man by her side
Hang on, she'll take you for a ride
Have another drink and smoke
Your feelings to her are a joke

But things aren't what they seem to be
As she fights not to be lonely
Drunk nights and tired days
Start to take her beauty away
She tries to hide the pain
But her children too, feel the shame

Late at night she cries to me
But not changing her reality
I did everything I could do
Can't let her lifestyle wreck me too
She's a tough girl, going to do it her way
Nothing you can do but break away

Small Town Circles

Don't care about right or wrong
Got to party all night long

Lonely lovers' give and take
Seems like every one is on the make

So Charles hits another home run
And big Jim always carries his gun

Back at the local bar, looking for fun
More drinks and drugs to come

Doing it all again the very next day
Thinking there's got to be another way

Small town circles go round and round
Can't let them put you in the ground

Sometimes

With all that we went through
There was still nothing else to do
Sorry won't work this time
Once you cross the bottom line
It doesn't matter who is right or wrong
It's just time we move on

Sometimes:
You have to lose a finger to save a hand
Leave that woman to be a man
Break your heart to save your soul
Take the pain then let it go!

No one's fault but yours and mine
There's no guilt to feel this time
Spreading lies to hurt my name
Does it really ease the pain?
Forgiveness is all that's left, you see
Let me go with my dignity

Sometimes:
You have to lose a finger to save a hand
Leave that woman to be a man
Break your heart to save your soul
Take the pain then let it go!

Old Love

I choose to leave
So I could breathe

Much of the past
On broken glass

And now you're here
Sad face and a tear

Your heart has turned
But bridges were burned

No looking back for me
Time only to break free

Can't get back yesterday
Old love just walk away

Ready to Die

The needle sticks again
Can't be near the end

The medicine holds me down
The bed keeps spinning around

Am I dreaming or awake
How much pain can I take

Falling into the abyss
Time is my only wish

Will take the last breath
Spitting in the face of death

Cannot shut my eyes
Not yet ready to die

Quotes

ANGER	Where mistakes breed and multiply like the locust
ARTIST	The risk one takes between working for survival or creating happiness
BEST	We all strive to be the best knowing it will only be temporary
CHARITY	Strive not to be a pillar of strength to the masses, rather a source of comfort to the downtrodden few
DEATH	Death is not the winner, yet an unhappy life the sinner
DEPRESSION	Sometimes we must walk through our own darkness to find the light in others
FATHERHOOD	My purpose secure, my life blessed
FRIENDSHIP	Friendship is tested most during times of poverty
GUILT	After a mistake, apologize then move forward fast or guilt will pin you to your past
KNOWLEDGE	Discipline without knowledge merely creates a slave
LONELINESS	Where negative thoughts destroy the mind
LOST LOVE	A weak heat has this strong man

MONEY	Money turns and twists me until all good has shaken loose
MOTHERS LOVE	Always praises my accomplishments, always blind to my failures
NATURE	Those in love with nature add to nature's beauty
PARADISE	Paradise is not found on a map, but in your mind
REVENGE	Sometimes I am too weak to deny your temptation
RELIGION	Maybe its only reason for existence is to slow the human race from killing itself

My Little Hometown

We would ride on our bikes
Well into the dark
And play in the train engine
They left in the park

We made friends on paper routes
And walking on train tracks
And our parents knew each other
From many years back

While swimming at the river
We could swing from a tree
And somewhere in the water
Learn about the birds and the bees

And Friday night football
Was a must see
A rite of passage
For the champions soon to be

Then it was college or marriage
The only options we could see
And a short time later
Many would choose to leave

The popular girls put their hopes
With the farmer boys
The rest, factory workers
And credit cards for their toys

The bowling alley and softball field
Were the only games in town
And back at Tommy's bar
Dreams came tumbling down

We never had much of anything
But always had a blast
Not knowing the good ole days
Would go by so fast

The friendships we made
Such a long time ago
Turned out to be the best
That we would know

And of all the many places
I would choose to roam
I always made it back
To that place called home

So when it comes time
For that eternal rest
Remember a simple man
That did his best

And have my old friends
Carry me to the ground
In this place that I love
My little hometown

Made in the USA
Columbia, SC
18 April 2024

5ef316b0-8bba-44c5-b7b3-b5d5a6188a6bR01